The Ultimate Scottish Cookbook

Recipes as Fierce as a Scottish Clan

Table of Contents

Introduction 5

Breakfast... 7

    Scottish Porridge.. 8

    Tattie Scones 10

    Scotch Eggs 12

    Scones 15

    Scottish Pancakes - Pikelets 18

Beef... 20

    Beef Wellington 21

    Minced Collops 24

    Scottish Sausage Rolls 26

Lamb 29

    Scottish Shepherd's Pie 30

    Stovies 33

    Lamb in a Cherry Reduction Sauce 35

    Lamb Pastries - Forfar Bridies....................... 37

    Scottish Mince Pie... 39

    Haggis, Neeps and Tatties 42

Seafood 45

    Fish Pie 46

    Scotch Woodcock 49

    Salmon Patties 51

    Beer Battered Fish 54

    Baked Finnan Haddie 56

    Partan Bree – Scottish Crab Soup 58

    Tattie, Neep and Carrot Soup 60

    Scotch Broth 62

    Cullen Skink 64

    Cock-A-Leekie Stew 66

Chicken 68

    Chicken Bonnie Prince Charlie 69

Vegetarian 72

    Rarebit 73

Side Dishes 76

    Bubbles and Squeak – Potato and Cabbage Patties 77

    Bacon Clapshot 79

Desserts 81

    Scottish Shortbread 82

    Toffee 84

    Cranachan 86

    Clootie Dumpling 88

    Scottish Butter Tablet 91

Scottish Bannock 93

Oatmeal Shortbread Cookies 95

Introduction

Scotland's landscape has determined its tasty cuisine. The rich green hills help produce the best Angus beef and lamb. The rough seashore is filled with all types of seafood. And the fertile soil is ideal for growing potatoes, cabbage, turnips, and other vegetables. Scotland has some of the best produce anywhere.

Of course, the descendants of William Wallace do love their whiskey, and you'll find a few drops in many of the recipes in the Ultimate Scottish Cookbook. (Fact: the Scots export 40 bottles of whiskey every second.) You'll also find a recipe using Scotland's national dish – haggis.

Perhaps William Wallace had a sweet tooth, because the Scots sure love their dessert. Try all the sweets you find in this book. Queen Victoria was a big fan.

While the beloved Queen was rarely amused, your kids will love the names of some genuine Scottish dishes and will be begging for stovies, bridies, bubbles and squeak, Scotch woodcock, tattie, neep and carrot soup, and cock-a-leekie stew. Just don't tell them that these dishes are healthy! Make eating fun again with the recipes in the Ultimate Scottish Cookbook.

Breakfast

Scottish Porridge

It gets cold in Scotland, and a hot porridge is just the thing on a cold winter morning.

Cooking Time: 30 minutes

Servings: 4

Ingredients:

- 1 cup rolled oats
- ¼ tsp. salt
- 1 cup whole milk
- 1 tbsp. maple syrup

- ¼ cup raisins

Directions:

1. Add 3 cups of water to a pan and stir in the oats and salt.

2. Stir frequently for 20 minutes.

3. Pour in the milk and cook on low for 10 minutes.

4. Top each bowl with some maple syrup and raisings.

Tattie Scones

Serve these delicious potato scones with scrambled eggs and sliced smoked salmon.

Cooking Time: 28 minutes

Servings: 16

Ingredients:

Servings 16

- 1 lb. cooked potatoes
- 1 cup flour

- ¼ cup butter
- Salt and pepper to taste (go easy on the pepper)
- 2 tbsp. butter for frying

Directions:

1. Cook for potatoes in a pot of salted water for 20 minutes, until done. (Or, just use leftover mashed potatoes.)

2. Peel the potatoes and mash them.

3. Season with salt and pepper.

4. Stir in the butter and flour and combine.

5. Place the dough on a flat, floured surface.

6. Create 4 separate balls.

7. Flatten each ball to a ¼ inch thickness.

8. Use a fork to put holes on the top of each scone.

9. Heat 2 tbsp. butter.

10. Fry each scone for 4 minutes on each side.

11. Slice the scones into quarters.

Scotch Eggs

Serve these beauties for breakfast with some bacon or have them as a snack or appetizer. Endless possibilities. And the sauce is luscious.

Cooking Time: 35 minutes

Servings: 6

Ingredients:

Sauce

- ¾ cup mayonnaise
- 3 tbsp. spicy mustard
- 1 tbsp. sugar
- 1 tbsp. lemon juice
- Scotch Eggs
- 6 eggs
- 2 tbsp. flour
- 12 oz. ground pork sausage
- 2 tsp. sage
- ½ tsp. marjoram
- Salt and pepper to taste
- 2 beaten egg
- ½ cup Panko breadcrumbs
- 1 cup canola oil

Directions:

1. Combine the **Sauce** ingredients in a pan.

2. Stir until the mixture comes to a boil, 5 minutes, then remove from the heat.

3. Refrigerate for 15 minutes.

4. Place the eggs in a pan of boiling water and cook for 10 minutes.

5. Remove from heat and let cool.

6. Heat the oil in a deep fryer.

7. Peel the eggs and dust them with flour.

8. Combine the sausage, sage, marjoram, salt and pepper in a bowl.

9. Use your hands and fingers to wrap the eggs with the sausage mixture.

10. Roll each wrapped egg in the beaten eggs, then in the breadcrumbs.

11. Use a slotted spoon to place the eggs in the hot oil.

12. Fry for 5 minutes.

13. Remove the eggs using a slotted spoon and drain on paper towel.

14. Serve the Scotch eggs with the **Sauce**.

Scones

Enjoy these with butter and jam and a lovely cup of tea.

Cooking Time: 15 minutes

Servings: 14

Ingredients:

- 2 cups flour
- 1 ½ cups rolled oats
- 3 tbsp. sugar

- ½ tsp. maple syrup
- 1 tsp. cinnamon
- ½ tsp. nutmeg
- 1 ½ tbsp. baking powder
- Dash of salt
- ½ cup chopped walnuts
- 1 beaten egg
- 1/3 cup melted butter
- ¼ cup milk

Directions:

1. Preheat the oven to 425 degrees.

2. Coat a baking dish with non-stick spray.

3. In a large bowl, mix the flour, oats, sugar, maple, cinnamon, nutmeg, baking powder, salt, and walnuts.

4. Create a well in the middle.

5. Combine the egg, melted butter and milk in a separate bowl.

6. Drizzle the liquid into the well.

7. Stir to create a dough.

8. Use the dough to form 2 circles that are ½ inch thick.

9. Transfer the dough circles to the baking dish.

10. Use a knife to divide each circle into 8 separate wedges.

11. Bake for 15 minutes.

12. Break the wedges apart and serve while they are still warm.

Scottish Pancakes - Pikelets

These are actually more like thin crumpets in texture and very popular at teatime.

Cooking Time: 4 minutes per pancake

Servings: 5

Ingredients:

- 1 cup flour
- ¼ tbsp. vinegar
- ¼ cup corn syrup
- ¼ tsp. baking soda
- 1 tsp. cinnamon

- 1 tsp. vanilla extract
- 1 beaten egg
- ¾ cup milk
- 3 tbsp. butter

Directions:

1. Combine all ingredients except the butter in a bowl.

2. Melt the butter in a skillet.

3. Use ¼ cup batter for each pancake

4. Cook for 2 minutes, flip the pancake and cook 2 more minutes.

5. Serve with your favorite jam.

Beef

Beef Wellington

Several countries lay claim to Beef Wellington, but the Scottish Angus beef places it on top.

Cooking Time: 1 hour

Servings: 8

Ingredients:

- 2 lb. beef tenderloin
- Salt and pepper to taste
- ½ tsp. garlic powder

- 2 tbsp. mustard
- 2 tbsp. butter
- 1 chopped onion
- 1 cup sliced mushroom
- 10 prosciutto slices
- Salt and pepper to taste
- 1 package thawed package frozen puff pastry
- 1 beaten egg yolk
- 1 ½ cup beef broth
- 3 tbsp. red wine
- 2 tbsp. chopped shallots
- 1 tsp. red vinegar

Directions:

1. Preheat the oven 425 degrees

2. Season the beef with salt, pepper and garlic powder

3. Bake for 15 minutes. Set aside any pan juices.

4. Heat 2 tbsp. butter in a skillet and sauté the onion and mushrooms. Set aside.

5. Wrap the prosciutto slices around the beef and top with the onion/mushrooms.

6. Flatten the puff pastry and add the beef to the middle.

7. Seal up the puff pastry with moist fingers.

8. Transfer the beef to a baking dish.

9. Brush the puff pastry with the egg yolk.

10. Bake at 450 degrees for 10 minutes, then bake at 425 degrees for 25 minutes.

11. Set aside.

12. Heat up the reserved pan juices, beef broth, wine, shallots and vinegar.

13. Let boil for 10 minutes until the **Sauce** reduces.

14. Serve the **Sauce** over the beef.

Minced Collops

This is Scotland's version of Hamburger Helper. It's a delicious way to stretch your hamburger budget.

Cooking Time: 55 minutes

Servings: 4

Ingredients:

- 1 tbsp. olive oil
- 1 lb. ground beef
- 1 small diced onion
- 2 minced garlic cloves

- Salt and pepper to taste
- 2/3 cup steel-cut oats
- 1 ¼ cups beef broth
- ¼ cup red wine
- 1 tbsp. Worcestershire Sauce
- 12 slices of toasted bread

Directions:

1. Heat the olive oil in a skillet.

2. Add the ground beef, onion, garlic and season with salt and pepper.

3. Sauté for 10 minutes.

4. Add the oats and stir well.

5. Pour in the beef broth and red wine.

6. Bring the liquid to a boil.

7. Lower the heat and simmer for 30 minutes.

8. Serve with a slice of toast on each plate

Scottish Sausage Rolls

The British have their bangers and mash. Up north, they have these delectable sausage rolls. They can be eaten for breakfast. With some mashed potatoes and peas, they make a great lunch.

Cooking Time: 25 minutes

Serving: 24

Ingredients:

- 1 package puff pastry
- 1 lb. ground beef

- 1 diced onion
- Salt and pepper to taste
- ½ tsp. dill
- ½ tsp. nutmeg
- Dash of cayenne pepper
- 1 cup Panko breadcrumbs
- 1 egg white

Directions:

1. Preheat your oven to 400 degrees.

2. Combine the beef, onion, salt, pepper, dill, nutmeg, cayenne pepper and breadcrumbs in a bow.

3. Add ¼ cup of water and mix into the ingredients. Add more water as needed. You want a firm but moist consistency.

4. Cut the puff pastry into 24 rectangles.

5. Divide the beef mixture between the pastry sheet.

6. Create log-shaped rolls.

7. Crimp the edges of the rolls shut with dampened fingers.

8. Transfer the rolls to a baking sheet lined with aluminum foil.

9. Whisk the egg white and brush some on each piece of pastry.

10. Bake for 25 minutes.

Lamb

Scottish Shepherd's Pie

This makes a homey dinner and a great use of leftover mashed potatoes.

Cooking Time: 40 minutes

Servings: 3

Ingredients:

- 1 tbsp. butter
- 1 lb. ground lamb
- 1 chopped onion
- 2 cups corn

- 2 cups frozen peas
- Salt and pepper to taste
- ½ cup beef broth
- 2 lb. mashed potatoes
- 3 tbsp. sour cream
- 2 tbsp. butter
- 2 tbsp. flour
- 1 cup grated cheddar cheese

Directions:

1. Preheat oven to 350 degrees.

2. Melt the butter in a skillet and brown the lamb and onion for 5 minutes.

3. Add the corn the peas and stir in the flour.

4. Season with the salt and pepper.

5. Cook for 5 minutes.

6. Place the mixture in a casserole dish.

7. Pour in the beef broth.

8. Bake for 10 minutes.

9. Combine the mashed potatoes, sour cream and butter.

10. Spread the mixture on top of the casserole.

11. Bake for 15 minutes.

12. Top with the grated cheese.

13. Bake for another 5 minutes.

Stovies

A comfort dish with potatoes and lamb. It's traditionally served on St. Andrew's Day.

Cooking Time: 30 minutes

Servings: 4

Ingredients:

- 6 peeled and cubed potatoes
- ¾ cup beef broth
- 2 tbsp. butter

- 1 diced onion
- ¾ lb. lamb chunks
- Salt and pepper to taste

1/8 tsp. nutmeg

Directions:

1. Combine the potatoes and broth in a pan.

2. Bring the broth to a boil, then simmer for 20 minutes.

3. Melt the butter in a skillet and sauté the onions for 5 minutes.

4. Stir in the onion and lamb into the potatoes.

5. Cook for 10 minutes.

6. Season with salt, pepper and nutmeg.

Lamb in a Cherry Reduction Sauce

Lamb in a lovely, savory **Sauce**. Serve with mash potatoes

Cooking Time: 50 minutes

Servings: 6

Ingredients:

- 1 cup port wine
- ½ cup balsamic vinegar
- ½ cup cherry juice
- 3 tbsp. chopped onion
- 2 minced garlic cloves
- 2 lb. rack of lamb
- Salt and pepper to taste

- 4 cups chicken broth
- 2 tbsp. butter
- Salt and pepper to taste

Directions:

1. Combine the port, vinegar, cherry juice, onion and garlic in a small pan.

2. Cook on medium up to reduce the **Sauce**, 10 minutes.

3. Stir in the stock and keep cooking until the **Sauce** is reduced by half.

4. Swirl in the butter.

5. Season the **Sauce** with salt and pepper. Keep the **Sauce** warm.

6. Preheat the oven to 350.

7. Season the lamb with salt and pepper and place on a baking sheet.

8. Bake for 20 minutes.

9. Drizzle the lamb with the **Sauce**.

Lamb Pastries - Forfar Bridies

Delicious meat pastries. Lamb is the traditional Scottish way to prepare this dish, but you can other meat if you prefer.

Cooking Time: 40 minutes

Servings: 8

- 1 tbsp. olive oil
- ¾ lb. ground lamb
- 1 chopped onion
- 1 large peeled and cubed potato
- 5 tbsp. beef broth
- 1 tbsp. Worcestershire **Sauce**

- Salt and pepper to taste
- ½ tsp. thyme
- 2 sheets puff pastry
- 1 egg white

Directions:

1. Preheat oven to 350 degrees.

2. Heat the oil in a skillet and brown the meat for 5 minutes. Drain the grease.

3. Stir in the onion, potatoes, broth, Worcestershire **Sauce**, salt, pepper and thyme.

4. Remove the skillet from the heat.

5. Cut the puff pastry into 4 pieces.

6. Fill each piece with equal amounts of filling.

7. Fold the puff pastry and brush with some egg white.

8. Transfer the puff pastry to a baking dish.

9. Bake for 35 minutes.

Scottish Mince Pie

This is definitely not a dessert pie. It's a hearty meat pie. Serve it with potatoes.

Cooking Time: 1 hour

Servings: 8

Ingredients:

- 1 ½ lb. ground lamb
- 1 cup of beer
- 1 diced onion

- 3 minced garlic cloves
- 1 tsp. Worcestershire **Sauce**
- 1 cup beef broth
- 1 cup sliced mushrooms
- Salt and pepper to taste
- 2 tablespoons cornstarch
- 2 frozen pie crusts

Directions:

1. Add the lamb and beer to a pot. Make sure the meat is covered with the liquid.

2. Boil for 10 minutes until the beef is done. Drain any remaining liquid.

3. Stir in the onion, garlic, Worcestershire **Sauce**, broth, mushroom, salt and pepper.

4. Stir the cornstarch into ¼ cup of water.

5. Stir the cornstarch into the lamb mixture.

6. Preheat the oven to 375 degrees.

7. Place one pie crust into a pie plate.

8. Add the lamb mixture.

9. Top with the second pie crust and close the edges

10. Bake for 50 minutes.

Haggis, Neeps and Tatties

This is a traditional meal to celebrate Burns Night.

Cooking Time: 1 hour 10 minutes

Servings: 4

Ingredients:

- ¾ lb. of prepared haggis – can be bought
- 4 large potatoes
- ½ cup butter
- ½ cup heavy cream
- 1 turnip
- 1 diced onion
- 1 cup sugar

- Dash of salt
- 2 minced garlic cloves
- 1 cup red wine
- 2 ½ cups chicken stock
- 1 tbsp. whiskey
- 3 tbsp. heavy cream

Directions:

1. Heat the olive oil in a skillet.

2. Sauté the onion for 5 minutes

3. Bake the potatoes until they are done – 45 minutes, depending on size.

4. Peel the potatoes and rice them.

5. Stir the sautéed onion, cream and butter into the potatoes. Keep warm.

6. Cook the turnip in salty water for 30 minutes until done.

7. Peel and rice the turnip. Keep warm

8. Cook the haggis according to instructions.

9. Create 3 layers of haggis, turnip and mashed potatoes in a baking dish.

10. To create the **Sauce**, combine the wine, sugar, garlic and salt.

11. Simmer for 5 minutes.

12. Stir in the chicken broth, heavy cream and whiskey.

13. Serve with the Sauce.

Seafood

Fish Pie

This simple dish goes well with a nice, green salad.

Cooking Time: 45 minutes

Servings: 6

- 1 tbsp. olive oil
- 2 sliced onions
- 5 peeled and cubed potatoes
- 8 oz. cubed salmon
- 10 oz. cubed cod
- 2 tbsp. butter
- 2 tbsp. flour
- 2 cups milk

- 1 cup heavy cream
- 1 tbsp. mustard
- 1 ½ cups grated Emmental cheese
- Salt and pepper to taste

Directions:

1. Preheat your oven to 350 degrees.

2. Then coat a 13x9 inch baking dish with non-stick spray.

3. Heat the oil in a skillet over medium heat.

4. Sauté the onion for 5 minutes.

5. Place the potatoes in a pot of boiling water and cook for 10 minutes, until done.

6. Place the potatoes in a baking dish.

7. Top the potatoes with the salmon and cod.

8. Use the same skillet to melt the butter and stir in the flour.

9. Keep stirring until you have a paste.

10. Add the milk and heavy cream.

11. Simmer while frequently stirring until you have a thick **Sauce**.

12. Season with the salt and pepper.

13. Remove the skillet from the heat.

14. Stir in the cheese.

15. Once the cheese is melted, add the **Sauce** to the baking dish making sure the potatoes and fish are covered.

16. Bake for 30 minutes.

Scotch Woodcock

Anchovy lovers unite! Queen Victoria, who spent a lot of time in Scotland, used to serve this after dinner. What a wild woman she was!

Cooking Time: 10 minutes

Servings: 4

Ingredients:

- 1 can anchovy fillets drained of all oil
- ¼ cup butter, separated
- 2 slices of bread
- 3 eggs

- 2 tbsp heavy cream
- Salt and pepper to taste
- Dash of cayenne pepper

Directions:

1. Open the anchovy can and keep four fillets in reserve.

2. Mash the remaining anchovies into 2 tbsp. butter and combine into a paste.

3. Toast the bread slices and cover with the anchovy paste.

4. Whisk the eggs and heavy cream.

5. Season with salt, pepper and cayenne pepper

6. Heat the other 2 tbsp. butter in a skillet and add the eggs. Scramble them until they are done but still soft, 4 minutes.

7. Top each slice of toast with some scrambled eggs.

8. Add 1 reserved anchovy fillet on top of each.

Salmon Patties

Scotland has some great salmon fishing. Try these traditional salmon patties with a nice salad.

Cooking Time: 27 minutes

Servings: 4

Ingredients:

- ¾ lb. cubed potatoes
- 3 salmon fillets
- 1 tsp. mustard

- 1 tsp. lemon zest
- ½ tsp. lemon pepper
- 1 tbsp. dill
- ¼ cup flour
- 1 beaten egg
- ½ cup Panko breadcrumb
- ¼ cup vegetable oil

Directions:

1. Boil the potatoes in salted water for 12 minutes or until done.

2. Drain and mash the potatoes.

3. Heat a grill and grill the salmon fillets for 5 minutes. They should be flaky.

4. Let cool and flake the salmon.

5. Add the potatoes, mustard, lemon zest and dill to the flaked salmon in a bowl.

6. Create 4 fishcakes.

7. Place the flour, egg, and Panko in separate dishes.

8. Dredge the salmon cakes through the flour, egg, and Panko.

9. Heat the vegetable oil in a skillet.

10. Fry the salmon cakes 5 minutes per side.

Beer Battered Fish

Scotland shares the same abundant sea with England, and both countries love their crispy battered cod. With chips, of course.

Cooking Time: 5 minutes

Servings: 8

Ingredients:

- 2 cups vegetable oil
- 8 cod fillets
- 2 egg whites

- 1 cup flour plus ¼ cup for dusting
- Salt and pepper to taste
- 1 tsp. onion powder
- 1 cup beer

Directions:

1. Heat the oil in a large skillet or keep fryer. The oil should get very hot.

2. Combine 1 cup flour, 2 egg whites, salt, pepper, onion powder and beer in a bowl.

3. Refrigerate the mixture for 2 hours.

4. Make sure your fish fillets are dry; dust them with ¼ cup of flour.

5. Coat the fish with the batter.

6. Carefully place the fish fillet in the hot oil using a tong.

7. Fry the fillets for 5 minutes while turning them once or twice while frying.

8. Serve with lemon slices and tartar **Sauce**.

Baked Finnan Haddie

Smoked fish is very popular in Scotland, and this is one of their favorite dishes.

Cooking Time: 35 minutes

Servings: 6

Ingredients:

- 1 sliced onion
- 2 lbs. smoked haddock fillets
- 3 tbsp. flour

- 5 tbsp. melted butter
- 2 cups warm milk
- 1 cup grated Irish cheese
- 1 tsp. mustard

Directions:

1. Preheat the oven to 325 degrees.

2. Place the onion slices in a baking dish

3. Arrange the fillets on top of the onions.

4. Whisk together the flour and butter.

5. Stir in the milk and mustard.

6. Gradually add the cheese and stir until smooth.

7. Pour the mixture over the fillets.

8. Bake for 35 minutes.

Soups

Partan Bree – Scottish Crab Soup

The harsh Scottish coastline is teeming with crabs. Use them in this delicious soup.

Cooking Time: 20 minutes

Servings: 4

Ingredients:

- 1 large cooked crab
- 1/3 cup rice
- 2 ¾ cups milk
- 1 cup fish stock

- ¾ cup heavy cream
- Salt and pepper to taste
- 1 tsp. lemon juice
- Finely chopped chives

Directions:

1. Pick all the meat from the crab and separate the meat from the claws.

2. Pour the milk in a pan and add the rice.

3. Cook for 10 minutes until the rice is done.

4. Drain the rice.

5. Chop the crab meat.

6. Add the crab meat, fish stock and heavy cream and heat the mixture.

7. Season with salt, pepper and lemon juice.

8. Let simmer for 5 minutes.

9. Add the crab claws and simmer for another 5 minutes.

10. Garnish with the chives.

Tattie, Neep and Carrot Soup

Serve this root vegetable soup with a hearty crusty bread. If you want a smooth soup, place the soup in a blender and puree until smooth.

Cooking Time: 45 minutes

Servings: 8

Ingredients:

- 1 tbsp butter
- 1 chopped onion
- 5 peeled and chopped carrots

- 1 chopped turnip
- 3 cubed large potatoes
- 8 cups chicken broth
- Salt and pepper to taste
- ½ tsp. ground coriander
- 8 tbsp. (2 cups) heavy cream
- ½ cup chopped parsley

Directions:

1. Melt the butter in a pot and sauté the onion for 5 minutes.

2. Stir in the potatoes, turnip and carrots and cook for 5 minutes.

3. Pour in the broth and season with salt, pepper and coriander.

4. Bring the broth to a boil, then simmer for 35 minutes.

5. Pour into bowls and add in a tbsp. heavy cream to each.

6. Top with chopped parsley

Scotch Broth

A bit of work goes into this broth, but it's well worth it.

Cooking Time: 3 hours 45 minutes

Servings: 8

Ingredients:

- 2 ½ lb. leg of lamb
- 8 cups low-sodium chicken broth
- 3 chopped onions
- 3 minced garlic cloves
- Salt and pepper to taste
- ½ tsp. oregano

- ½ tsp. thyme
- ½ cup barley
- 3 peeled and sliced carrots
- 1 cleaned and chopped leek
- 2 chopped turnips
- 1/3 cup chopped parsley

Directions:

1. Place the lamb, onions, garlic, salt, pepper, oregano and thyme in a soup pot.

2. Bring to a boil, then simmer for 3 hours.

3. Transfer the lamb to a plate and shred or chop.

4. Return the meat to the pot and refrigerate overnight.

5. Skim off any surface fat.

6. Soak the barley in water for 1 hour.

7. Reheat the stock and add the barley and vegetables.

8. Let the broth boil, then reduce to a simmer for 35 minutes.

9. Garnish with parsley.

Cullen Skink

You might not guess by the name, but this is a thick and rich seafood chowder. Cullen is actually a coastal town by the Irish Sea.

Cooking Time: 30 minutes

Servings: 4

Ingredients:

- 2 lb. flounder
- 2 ½ cups milk
- ¼ cup white wine

- 2 cups peeled and diced potatoes
- 1 chopped onion
- Salt and pepper to taste
- 1 tsp. liquid smoke

Directions:

1. Add the flounder, milk and wine in a pan and simmer for 10 minutes.

2. Use a slotted spoon to transfer the flounder to a plate.

3. Stir the potatoes, onion, salt, pepper and liquid smoke into the milk and simmer for 15 minutes.

4. Use a blender to process all or part of the potato mixture, depending on how smooth you want the chowder.

5. Flake the fish.

6. Return the blended potato mixture to the pan and stir in the fish.

7. Simmer for 5 minutes to heat.

Cock-A-Leekie Stew

This is a Scottish version of chicken soup. The prunes are traditional and add a nice sweetness.

Cooking Time: 1 hour 5 minutes

Servings: 4

Ingredients:

- 3 lb. chicken cut into large pieces
- ½ cup sliced carrots
- 1 cup barley
- 1 cup sliced mushrooms

- 4 cups chicken stock
- Salt and pepper to taste
- ½ tsp. poultry seasoning
- 1 cleaned and sliced leek
- 1 cup of diced prunes

Directions:

1. Add the chicken, carrots, mushrooms, barley, broth, salt, pepper and poultry seasoning to a pot.

2. Combine and bring the broth to a boil.

3. Reduce the heat to a simmer and cook for 50 minutes.

4. Add the leeks and simmer for 15 more minutes.

5. Add the chopped prunes to the soup bowls and ladle the soup.

Chicken

Chicken Bonnie Prince Charlie

OK, the Scots tried to get Bonnie Prince Charles on the throne of England. They failed, but they did name a chicken after him. The Drambuie is an integral part of the **Sauce**, so don't omit it or exchange it.

Cooking Time: 31 minutes

Servings: 6

Ingredients:

- 6 boneless chicken breasts
- ¼ cup flour

- Salt and pepper to taste
- 3 tbsp. vegetable oil.
- ¼ cup Drambuie
- ¼ cup chicken broth
- 3 large apples, peeled, cored and sliced
- 1 ¼ cup heavy cream
- ¼ cup chopped and toasted almonds

Directions:

1. Combine the flour, salt, and pepper in a bowl.

2. Dredge the chicken through the flour.

3. Heat the oil and fry the chicken on both sides for 8 minutes each side.

4. Drain the chicken on a paper towel and clean the skillet.

5. Drizzle the Drambuie over the chicken.

6. Return the chicken to the skillet and pour in the chicken broth.

7. Cover the skillet and let the chicken simmer for 10 minutes.

8. Melt the butter in another skillet.

9. Add the apple slices and cook until soft, 8 minutes.

10. Transfer the chicken to a platter and keep warm.

11. Add the cooked apples to the platter.

12. Stir the heavy cream into the chicken broth. If needed, add a bit more Drambuie.

13. Warm the **Sauce** but don't bring to a boil.

14. Stir in the almonds and simmer for 5 minutes.

15. Top the chicken with the **Sauce** and serve with the cooked apples.

Vegetarian

Rarebit

Scottish rarebit has a bit more zip (thanks to the beer and whiskey), than its more famous Welsh counterpart. If you want to cross the border to Wales, just substitute milk for the beer. Rarebit isn't just for serving over toast. Living up your favorite vegetables with this great **Sauce**.

Cooking Time: 16 minutes

Servings: 6

Ingredients:

- ¼ cup butter
- 3 tbsp. diced onion
- 1/3 cup flour
- Salt and pepper to taste
- ½ tsp. mustard
- ¼ tsp. Worcestershire Sauce
- Dash of cayenne pepper
- 1 cup whole milk
- ¾ cup stout – different beers will change the taste slightly
- 2 cups shredded cheddar cheese
- 6 slices sourdough bread

Directions:

1. Melt the butter in a large skillet.

2. Sauté the onions for 5 minutes.

3. Stir in the flour, pepper, salt, mustard, cayenne pepper and Worcestershire **Sauce**.

4. Keep stirring for 5 minutes until the mixture is smooth.

5. Pour in the milk and continue stirring until the milk boils, 4 minutes.

6. Add the beer and stir for another minute.

7. Stir in the cheese until it melts, 2 minutes.

8. Toast the sourdough bread slices.

9. Pour the cheese mixture over the toast.

Side Dishes

Bubbles and Squeak – Potato and Cabbage Patties

These patties are delicious, and how can your kids resist anything called Bubbles and Squeak? Use leftover mashed potatoes for extra ease in preparation.

Cooking Time: 25 minutes

Servings: 4

- 1 lb. peeled and cubed potatoes or use leftover mashed potatoes
- 2 cups prepared coleslaw mix
- 2 tbsp. butter
- 1 diced onion

- 2 minced garlic cloves
- 1 cup chopped ham
- Salt and pepper to taste
- ¾ cup shredded Cheddar cheese
- 2 tbsp. olive oil

Directions:

1. Cook the potatoes in a pot of salted water for 10 minutes.

2. Drain the potatoes and mash them. Set aside.

3. Heat the butter in a skillet.

4. Sauté the coleslaw, onion, garlic for 5 minutes.

5. Stir in the chopped ham.

6. Add the mashed potatoes and grated cheese and combine well.

7. Season with salt and pepper.

8. Create 4 patties.

9. Fry each patty for 5 minutes on each side.

Bacon Clapshot

A delicious potato side dish from Northern Scotland. For a slightly different taste sensation, try substituting rutabaga for the turnips. It's not traditional, but it's deliciously different. The idea is to bring a bit of tang to ordinary mashed potatoes.

Cooking Time: 15 minutes

Servings: 6

Ingredients:

- 1 ¼ lb. peeled and cubed potatoes
- ¾ lb. peeled and cubed turnips
- 1 chopped small onion
- ¼ cup butter

- ¼ cup chicken broth
- 6 cooked bacon strips
- Dash of whiskey
- Salt and pepper to taste
- 3 tbsp. chopped scallions

Directions:

1. Place the potatoes and turnips in a pan of boiling water and cook for 15 minutes, until done. Drain.

2. Mash both vegetables and stir in the butter and chicken broth. Stir well or use a hand mixer.

3. Stir in the whiskey and season with salt and pepper.

4. Add the scallion and crumbled bacon before serving.

Desserts

Scottish Shortbread

Scottish Shortbread isn't overly sweet. It is merely perfectly satisfying with a cup of coffee or tea. Its buttery taste makes it everyone's favorite.

Cooking Time: 20 minutes

Servings: 24

Ingredients:

- 2 cups softened butter
- 1 cup brown sugar
- ½ tsp. almond extract

- 4 cups flour
- Dash of salt

Directions:

1. Preheat the oven to 325 degrees.

2. Cream the butter, sugar and almond extract in a bowl.

3. Combine the flour and the salt and add to the mixture.

4. Dust a flat surface with the remaining flour.

5. Knead lightly for 5 minutes.

6. Place the dough in a baking dish and flatten to a half-inch thickness.

7. Cut the dough into 3-inch strips.

8. Bake at 325 degrees for 20 minutes but check at 15 minutes.

9. For added panache, drizzle the shortbread with melted dark chocolate

Toffee

Double chocolate toffee – so yummy. These make ideal holiday presents.

Cooking Time: 15 minutes

Servings: 16

Ingredients:

- 1/3 cup softened butter
- ¾ cup brown sugar
- Dash of sea salt
- 1 tsp of vanilla extract

- ½ cup of milk chocolate
- ½ cup semisweet chocolate chips
- 2 cups quick-cooking oats

Directions:

1. Preheat the oven to 400 degrees.

2. Grease a 9-inch baking dish

3. Thoroughly combine the butter and oats.

4. Stir in the sugar, salt and vanilla extract

5. Melt the milk chocolate in the microwave.

6. Pour the melted milk chocolate into the dish.

7. Add the mixture on top.

8. Bake for 12 minutes and let cool.

9. Melt the semisweet chocolate in the microwave.

10. Drizzle the toffee with the semisweet chocolate

11. Let cool and cut into pieces.

Cranachan

This creamy concoction is a very traditional Scottish dessert. Enjoy.

Cooking Time: 10 minutes.

Servings: 4

Ingredients:

- 2/3 cup rolled oats
- 1 ¼ cup double cream
- 2 tbsp. honey
- 5 tbsp. confectioners' sugar

- 1 tsp. vanilla extract
- 1 cup fresh raspberries
- 2 tsp. Scottish whiskey

Directions:

1. Preheat the oven to 350 degrees.

2. Spread the oats on a baking sheet and bake for 10 minutes.

3. Let the oats cool.

4. Whisk the double cream and honey in a bowl until stiff.

5. Fold in the sugar, vanilla and oats.

6. Divide the mixture into four bowls.

7. Spoon the raspberries over each mixture.

8. Drizzle with Scottish whiskey.

Clootie Dumpling

This is a traditional steamed Scottish dessert, filled with fruits and spices.

Cooking Time: 3 hours 45 minutes

Servings: 8

Ingredients:

- 4 cups flour
- ¾ cup dried currants
- ¾ cup chopped dates
- 1 cups raisin
- ¼ lb. shredded suet
- ¾ cup breadcrumbs

- ¾ cup brown sugar
- 1 beaten egg
- ¾ cup milk
- ¼ tsp. nutmeg
- ¼ tsp. cinnamon
- ¼ tsp. cloves
- 1 tsp. baking powder
- Dash of salt
- 1 tbsp. treacle
- 1 cup clotted cream

Directions:

1. Fill a pot with water and bring to a boil.

2. Stir the flour, currants, dates, raisin, suet, breadcrumbs and sugar into a bowl.

3. Combine the egg, milk, nutmeg, allspice, baking powder, salt and treacle in a second bowl.

4. Stir the egg mixture into the flour/fruit mixture.

5. Dampen a cloth with some boiling water.

6. Knead the dough into a ball.

7. Place the dough into the dampened cloth and tie with a twist or string.

8. Insert the dough into the boiling water

9. Cook for 3 ½ hours on a low boil

10. Heat to oven to 150 degrees.

11. Place the dough on a baking sheet and let dry in the oven for 15 minutes.

12. Serve with clotted cream.

Scottish Butter Tablet

These have a wonderful caramel taste.

Cooking Time: 25 minutes

Servings: 10

Ingredients:

- 2 cups sweetened condensed milk
- 1 cup heavy cream
- ¼ white sugar
- ¼ brown sugar
- 1 tbsp. corn syrup

- ½ cup cold cubed butter
- ¼ tsp. salt
- 1 tsp. vanilla extract

Directions:

1. Grease a 13 x 18 baking sheet.

2. Combine all ingredients in a pan.

3. Bring to boil over medium heat while stirring.

4. Reduce the heat to a simmer.

5. Stir until a candy thermometer reads 240 degrees, about 20 minutes.

6. Remove the pan from the heat and beat vigorously for 5 minutes.

7. Pour the mixture into the baking sheet.

8. Let the mixture cool.

9. Refrigerate overnight.

10. Cut into 10 pieces.

Scottish Bannock

This is a wonderful sweet bread. Rumor has it that it was one of Queen Victoria's favorites when she was in Scotland.

Cooking Time: 15 minutes

Servings: 12

Ingredients:

- 3 cups flour
- ½ tsp. salt
- 1 tsp. cinnamon
- 2 tbsp. baking powder

- ¼ cup melted lard
- ¾ cups raisins
- ½ tbsp. butter

Directions:

1. Combine the flour, salt, cinnamon and baking powder in a bowl.

2. Stir in the melted lard and 1 cup of water.

3. Add the raisins to the dough.

4. Place the dough on a floured surface and knead for 10 minutes.

5. Create a circle with a 1-inch thickness.

6. Melt the butter in a skillet.

7. Fry the bread 15 minutes each side on medium heat.

Oatmeal Shortbread Cookies

Relax, sit back, and have a steaming cuppa with these delicious cookies.

Cooking Time: 15 minutes

Servings: 12

Ingredients:

- 1 tsp. baking soda
- 3 cups rolled oats
- 1 cup flour
- ¾ cup brown sugar
- 1 cup chilled butter
- ½ tsp. salt

- ½ tsp. cinnamon
- ½ tsp. nutmeg
- 1 tsp. vanilla

Directions:

1. Preheat the oven to 375 degrees.

2. Add the baking soda to 3 tbsp. of water.

3. Combined the oats, flour and sugar in a bowl.

4. Cut the butter into the mixture until it is coarse.

5. Stir in the salt, cinnamon, nutmeg and vanilla.

6. Add the baking soda mix and combine well.

7. Create a dough ball.

8. Place the dough on a flat surface and roll it to ¼ inch thickness.

9. Place the dough in a 9x13 baking pan.

10. Bake at 375 degrees for 15 minutes.

11. Let cool and cut into oblong pieces.

Printed in Great Britain
by Amazon